EMMANUEL JOSEPH

Saintly Startups, Encouraging Faith, Ethics, and Innovation in Young Minds

Copyright © 2025 by Emmanuel Joseph

All rights reserved. No part of this publication may be reproduced, stored or transmitted in any form or by any means, electronic, mechanical, photocopying, recording, scanning, or otherwise without written permission from the publisher. It is illegal to copy this book, post it to a website, or distribute it by any other means without permission.

First edition

This book was professionally typeset on Reedsy.
Find out more at reedsy.com

Contents

1. Chapter 1: The Genesis of Saintly Startups — 1
2. Chapter 2: The Ethical Entrepreneur's Handbook — 3
3. Chapter 3: Faith and Innovation: The Perfect Synergy — 4
4. Chapter 4: The Power of Community — 5
5. Chapter 5: Overcoming Challenges with Grace — 6
6. Chapter 6: The Role of Mentorship — 7
7. Chapter 7: Faith-Driven Financial Models — 8
8. Chapter 8: The Impact of Technology — 9
9. Chapter 9: Cultivating a Culture of Innovation — 10
10. Chapter 10: Building Sustainable Businesses — 11
11. Chapter 11: Cultivating Empathy in Leadership — 13
12. Chapter 12: The Role of Faith in Business Decisions — 14
13. Chapter 13: Nurturing the Next Generation — 15
14. Chapter 14: Celebrating Successes — 16
15. Chapter 15: The Legacy of Saintly Startups — 17
16. Chapter 16: Embracing Diversity — 18
17. Chapter 17: The Role of Education — 19
18. Chapter 18: Balancing Business and Personal Life — 20
19. Chapter 19: The Importance of Resilience — 21
20. Chapter 20: Social Entrepreneurship — 22
21. Chapter 21: Building Strong Partnerships — 23
22. Chapter 22: The Role of Faith-Based Networks — 24
23. Chapter 23: Ethical Marketing Practices — 25
24. Chapter 24: Measuring Impact — 26
25. Chapter 25: The Future of Saintly Startups — 27

1

Chapter 1: The Genesis of Saintly Startups

In the bustling town of Suleja, nestled between the hustle of commerce and the serenity of its ancient traditions, a revolution in entrepreneurship was brewing. It wasn't the kind of revolution driven by sheer profits or market domination. No, this was a revolution of the spirit—a saintly spark ignited within the hearts of young, ambitious minds. Young Musa, a dreamer with a heart full of faith and a mind bursting with ideas, stood at the forefront. Unlike others, Musa saw his entrepreneurial journey as a divine calling, an opportunity to harmonize faith with the practicality of innovation.

Musa's early days were marked by his constant tussle with the norms. While many were skeptical of intertwining business with spirituality, Musa felt a profound need to prove that ethical entrepreneurship wasn't just a lofty ideal but a tangible reality. He started his journey by engaging with local artisans, ensuring fair trade practices and uplifting the community's spirit. Through storytelling sessions and local gatherings, he instilled a sense of purpose in those around him, painting a vivid picture of what a faith-driven startup could achieve.

One evening, while narrating the story of Prophet Solomon's wisdom and wealth, Musa captivated his small audience. He drew parallels between Solomon's fair dealings and the modern business world, emphasizing integrity over quick gains. This resonated deeply with young entrepreneurs, who saw in Musa's vision a path that was both righteous and rewarding. The seeds of Saintly Startups were thus sown, promising a future where faith and innovation could coexist harmoniously.

2

Chapter 2: The Ethical Entrepreneur's Handbook

Understanding the importance of a strong ethical foundation, Musa and his friends compiled an "Ethical Entrepreneur's Handbook." This was not just a guide on business practices but a manifesto of values, inspired by ancient wisdom and modern needs. They emphasized virtues such as honesty, transparency, compassion, and community service as the core pillars of their entrepreneurial journey.

Musa often shared the inspiring tale of his grandfather, a humble trader who never compromised on his values, even in the face of fierce competition. His grandfather's business may not have been the largest, but it was certainly the most respected. This narrative instilled in young entrepreneurs the realization that true success was measured not just in financial terms but also in the trust and respect one garnered from the community.

The handbook became a beacon of hope and guidance for many. It contained stories of historical figures, revered for their ethical conduct, and drew lessons from their lives. Each chapter was interspersed with real-life anecdotes from local entrepreneurs who had successfully implemented these values in their businesses. It became a cherished companion for aspiring entrepreneurs, reminding them that the path of integrity was not only noble but also immensely fulfilling.

3

Chapter 3: Faith and Innovation: The Perfect Synergy

Musa knew that for Saintly Startups to thrive, innovation had to go hand in hand with faith. He encouraged young entrepreneurs to think creatively while staying rooted in their ethical beliefs. This unique blend of faith and innovation gave rise to groundbreaking ideas that were both socially responsible and commercially viable.

He often narrated the story of Mariam, a young innovator who designed eco-friendly packaging inspired by traditional weaving techniques. Mariam's innovation not only reduced environmental waste but also provided a source of income for local weavers, preserving an ancient craft. Her startup, Green Weave, became a symbol of how faith-driven innovation could create sustainable solutions.

Mariam's story inspired others to think outside the box. From tech startups developing apps for community welfare to agricultural ventures employing sustainable practices, the Saintly Startups movement saw a wave of innovation that was deeply rooted in ethical principles. Faith was no longer seen as a limitation but as a guiding light, illuminating the path to responsible and impactful entrepreneurship.

4

Chapter 4: The Power of Community

One of the core tenets of Saintly Startups was the emphasis on community. Musa believed that businesses should not operate in isolation but as an integral part of the community, contributing to its growth and well-being. He encouraged young entrepreneurs to engage with their local communities, understand their needs, and create solutions that addressed those needs.

Musa's weekly community gatherings became a platform for knowledge sharing and collaboration. Entrepreneurs from different fields came together, shared their experiences, and brainstormed solutions to common challenges. These gatherings fostered a sense of camaraderie and mutual support, strengthening the bond between businesses and the community.

One particularly inspiring story was that of Amina, a social entrepreneur who started a cooperative for women artisans. Amina's initiative provided these women with the resources and training they needed to market their products effectively. Her cooperative not only empowered women but also revitalized the local economy, showcasing the transformative power of community-driven entrepreneurship.

5

Chapter 5: Overcoming Challenges with Grace

The journey of Saintly Startups was not without its challenges. Young entrepreneurs faced numerous obstacles, from financial constraints to market competition. However, what set them apart was their resilience and unwavering faith. They viewed challenges as opportunities for growth and learning, drawing strength from their ethical beliefs to overcome adversity.

Musa often recounted the story of Yusuf, a young farmer who faced a devastating drought. Instead of giving up, Yusuf turned to innovative irrigation techniques and sought the support of his community. With their help, he not only revived his farm but also set up a training center to educate other farmers on sustainable practices. Yusuf's perseverance became a beacon of hope for many, demonstrating that faith and determination could triumph over any obstacle.

Challenges were seen as stepping stones, propelling young entrepreneurs towards greater heights. They learned to navigate the complexities of the business world with grace and humility, never compromising on their values. Their journey was a testament to the fact that ethical entrepreneurship, though demanding, was incredibly rewarding.

6

Chapter 6: The Role of Mentorship

Recognizing the importance of guidance, Musa established a mentorship program where experienced entrepreneurs shared their wisdom with the younger generation. This program created a bridge between the old and the new, ensuring that the valuable lessons of the past were not lost but adapted to contemporary needs.

Mentors like Fatima, a seasoned entrepreneur with decades of experience, played a crucial role in shaping the future of Saintly Startups. Fatima's story was one of resilience and adaptability. She had successfully navigated numerous business cycles, adapting her strategies to changing market conditions while staying true to her values. Her insights were invaluable, providing young entrepreneurs with practical advice and moral support.

The mentorship program fostered a culture of continuous learning and improvement. It created a supportive environment where young entrepreneurs felt encouraged to take risks, innovate, and grow. The wisdom of the mentors, combined with the fresh perspectives of the young minds, created a powerful synergy that propelled the Saintly Startups movement forward.

7

Chapter 7: Faith-Driven Financial Models

One of the innovative aspects of Saintly Startups was the development of faith-driven financial models. Musa and his team understood that traditional financial models often did not align with their ethical principles. They sought to create alternative models that were fair, transparent, and inclusive.

Musa's friend, Ibrahim, played a pivotal role in this endeavor. An expert in Islamic finance, Ibrahim designed financial products that adhered to ethical guidelines while providing necessary support to startups. His models emphasized profit-sharing, risk mitigation, and community investment, ensuring that financial transactions were beneficial for all parties involved.

Ibrahim's story of creating a microfinance initiative for rural entrepreneurs was particularly inspiring. His initiative provided interest-free loans to small business owners, enabling them to grow their ventures without the burden of debt. This approach not only supported economic development but also fostered a sense of solidarity and mutual support within the community.

8

Chapter 8: The Impact of Technology

Technology played a crucial role in the success of Saintly Startups. Musa encouraged young entrepreneurs to leverage technology to enhance their businesses, reach wider audiences, and create impactful solutions. He emphasized the ethical use of technology, ensuring that it served the greater good and upheld the principles of fairness and transparency.

One standout story was that of Zainab, a tech enthusiast who developed an app to connect local artisans with global markets. Her app, Artisans Connect, provided a platform for artisans to showcase their products, reach international customers, and receive fair compensation for their work. Zainab's innovation not only boosted the artisans' incomes but also preserved cultural heritage and promoted ethical consumption.

Technology became a powerful enabler for Saintly Startups, breaking down barriers and creating new opportunities. From e-commerce platforms to digital marketing tools, young entrepreneurs harnessed the power of technology to amplify their impact and drive positive change. Their ethical approach to technology ensured that it was used responsibly and for the benefit of all.

9

Chapter 9: Cultivating a Culture of Innovation

Innovation was at the heart of Saintly Startups. Musa believed that fostering a culture of innovation was essential for the movement's success. He encouraged young entrepreneurs to think creatively, experiment with new ideas, and embrace failure as a learning opportunity.

One of the most memorable stories was that of Ahmed, a young inventor who developed a low-cost water purification device. Inspired by the need for clean drinking water in his community, Ahmed spent countless hours experimenting and refining his invention. His persistence paid off when his device gained widespread recognition and was adopted by communities across the region.

Ahmed's story exemplified the spirit of innovation that defined Saintly Startups. It highlighted the importance of perseverance, creativity, and a willingness to take risks. Musa and his team created an environment where young entrepreneurs felt empowered to explore new ideas and turn their visions into reality.

10

Chapter 10: Building Sustainable Businesses

Sustainability was a key focus for Saintly Startups. Musa and his team emphasized the importance of building businesses that were not only profitable but also environmentally and socially responsible. They encouraged young entrepreneurs to adopt sustainable practices and create solutions that addressed pressing global challenges.

One inspiring example was that of Fatima, a young entrepreneur who started a sustainable fashion brand. Fatima sourced eco-friendly materials, employed ethical manufacturing processes, and atima sourced eco-friendly materials, employed ethical manufacturing processes, and promoted conscious consumerism. Her brand, Ethos Fashion, gained popularity for its stylish yet sustainable designs. Fatima's commitment to sustainability extended beyond her products; she also invested in community initiatives such as tree-planting drives and educational workshops on environmental conservation.

Fatima's story inspired many young entrepreneurs to adopt sustainable practices in their own ventures. They realized that business success could go hand in hand with environmental stewardship, creating a positive impact on both the planet and society. The Saintly Startups movement became synonymous with sustainability, setting a new standard for responsible entrepreneurship.

11

Chapter 11: Cultivating Empathy in Leadership

Musa believed that true leadership was rooted in empathy and compassion. He encouraged young entrepreneurs to lead with their hearts, understanding the needs and concerns of their employees, customers, and communities. Empathy became a cornerstone of the Saintly Startups ethos, guiding leaders to make decisions that were fair and just.

One touching story was that of Hakeem, a startup founder who prioritized the well-being of his employees. When one of his team members faced a family crisis, Hakeem went above and beyond to provide support, offering flexible work arrangements and financial assistance. His compassionate approach created a positive work environment, fostering loyalty and dedication among his team.

Hakeem's story exemplified the power of empathetic leadership. It demonstrated that by valuing and caring for their people, leaders could build strong, resilient organizations. The Saintly Startups movement embraced this principle, creating a culture where empathy was not just an ideal but a daily practice.

12

Chapter 12: The Role of Faith in Business Decisions

Faith played a central role in guiding business decisions for Saintly Startups. Musa and his team believed that faith provided a moral compass, helping entrepreneurs navigate complex situations with integrity and wisdom. They encouraged young entrepreneurs to seek guidance from their faith traditions, drawing strength and inspiration from their beliefs.

One profound story was that of Aisha, a business owner who faced a tough decision regarding a lucrative but unethical partnership. Guided by her faith, Aisha chose to walk away from the deal, prioritizing her values over potential profits. Her decision, though challenging, earned her the respect and admiration of her peers and customers.

Aisha's story highlighted the importance of staying true to one's beliefs, even in the face of difficult choices. It reinforced the idea that faith could provide clarity and direction, helping entrepreneurs make decisions that were aligned with their principles. The Saintly Startups movement celebrated this integration of faith and business, showcasing the strength and resilience it brought to entrepreneurs.

13

Chapter 13: Nurturing the Next Generation

Musa and his team understood the importance of nurturing the next generation of ethical entrepreneurs. They established mentorship programs, workshops, and educational initiatives to inspire and empower young minds. These efforts aimed to create a pipeline of future leaders who would carry forward the values of Saintly Startups.

One inspiring story was that of Sara, a high school student who participated in one of the entrepreneurship workshops. Sara developed a business idea focused on recycling and waste management, addressing a pressing issue in her community. With guidance from her mentors, she turned her idea into a successful startup, setting an example for her peers.

Sara's story underscored the potential of young minds to drive positive change. It highlighted the importance of providing them with the tools and support they needed to succeed. The Saintly Startups movement became a beacon of hope for the next generation, fostering a sense of purpose and possibility.

14

Chapter 14: Celebrating Successes

The journey of Saintly Startups was marked by numerous successes, each one a testament to the power of faith, ethics, and innovation. Musa and his team made it a point to celebrate these successes, recognizing the achievements of young entrepreneurs and sharing their stories with the world.

One memorable celebration was the annual Saintly Startups Summit, where entrepreneurs from across the region gathered to showcase their ventures and share their experiences. The summit featured inspiring keynote speakers, interactive workshops, and networking opportunities, creating a vibrant and supportive community.

The story of the summit's keynote speaker, Bilal, was particularly inspiring. Bilal, a former mentee of Musa, had grown his tech startup into a successful enterprise that provided job opportunities for hundreds of young people. His journey from a budding entrepreneur to a seasoned leader was a testament to the power of perseverance and ethical leadership.

The summit became a platform for recognizing and celebrating the impact of Saintly Startups. It reinforced the idea that success was not just about financial gains but also about making a positive difference in the world. The stories shared at the summit inspired many to embark on their own entrepreneurial journeys, carrying forward the legacy of faith-driven innovation.

15

Chapter 15: The Legacy of Saintly Startups

As the years went by, the Saintly Startups movement left an indelible mark on the entrepreneurial landscape. Musa's vision of integrating faith, ethics, and innovation became a guiding light for many, shaping a new generation of entrepreneurs who prioritized integrity and social responsibility.

The legacy of Saintly Startups was evident in the thriving businesses that had sprouted across the region, each one a testament to the power of ethical entrepreneurship. These businesses not only contributed to economic growth but also uplifted communities, preserved cultural heritage, and addressed pressing social and environmental challenges.

Musa's story, from a young dreamer to a visionary leader, became a source of inspiration for many. His journey demonstrated that with faith, determination, and a commitment to ethical principles, it was possible to create businesses that were both successful and meaningful.

The Saintly Startups movement continued to grow, touching the lives of countless individuals and fostering a culture of responsible entrepreneurship. It became a beacon of hope, reminding everyone that the path to success was not just paved with profits but also with purpose, compassion, and integrity.

16

Chapter 16: Embracing Diversity

One of the hallmarks of Saintly Startups was its celebration of diversity. Musa and his team believed that embracing different perspectives, cultures, and backgrounds enriched the entrepreneurial journey. They encouraged young entrepreneurs to be inclusive, fostering an environment where everyone felt valued and respected.

An inspiring story was that of Kwame, a young entrepreneur from a different region who joined the Saintly Startups movement. Despite initial cultural differences, Kwame's unique ideas and experiences brought a fresh perspective to the community. His startup, Harmony Crafts, showcased traditional crafts from various cultures, promoting unity and appreciation for diversity.

Kwame's story highlighted the importance of inclusivity in entrepreneurship. It demonstrated that by embracing diversity, businesses could create more innovative solutions and build stronger communities. The Saintly Startups movement became a melting pot of ideas and cultures, enriching the entrepreneurial landscape.

17

Chapter 17: The Role of Education

Education was a cornerstone of the Saintly Startups movement. Musa and his team recognized that knowledge was the key to empowering young entrepreneurs and enabling them to succeed. They established partnerships with educational institutions, providing training programs, workshops, and resources to aspiring entrepreneurs.

One remarkable story was that of Zainab, a young woman who pursued higher education despite facing numerous challenges. With the support of Saintly Startups, Zainab received a scholarship to study business management. Upon graduation, she started her own venture, Empowered Women, which focused on providing educational opportunities for other young women.

Zainab's story underscored the transformative power of education. It showcased how access to knowledge and skills could empower individuals to achieve their dreams and make a positive impact on their communities. The Saintly Startups movement prioritized education, ensuring that young entrepreneurs had the tools they needed to thrive.

18

Chapter 18: Balancing Business and Personal Life

Balancing the demands of entrepreneurship with personal life was a challenge many young entrepreneurs faced. Musa and his team emphasized the importance of maintaining a healthy work-life balance, ensuring that entrepreneurs could pursue their passions without compromising their well-being.

One touching story was that of Karim, a dedicated entrepreneur who struggled to balance his startup with his family responsibilities. With guidance from his mentor, Karim learned to prioritize self-care and set boundaries. He implemented flexible work hours and invested in time-management techniques, allowing him to spend quality time with his family while growing his business.

Karim's story highlighted the importance of work-life balance in entrepreneurship. It demonstrated that with proper planning and support, entrepreneurs could achieve success without sacrificing their personal lives. The Saintly Startups movement promoted a holistic approach to entrepreneurship, valuing both professional achievements and personal well-being.

19

Chapter 19: The Importance of Resilience

Resilience was a defining characteristic of Saintly Startups. Musa and his team believed that the ability to bounce back from setbacks and persevere in the face of challenges was essential for entrepreneurial success. They encouraged young entrepreneurs to cultivate resilience and view failures as opportunities for growth.

One inspiring story was that of Amina, a young entrepreneur who faced multiple setbacks in her journey. Despite initial failures, Amina refused to give up. She sought feedback, made improvements, and eventually developed a successful online platform for local artisans. Her journey of resilience became a source of inspiration for many.

Amina's story showcased the power of perseverance and determination. It reinforced the idea that failures were not the end but rather stepping stones to success. The Saintly Startups movement celebrated resilience, encouraging entrepreneurs to learn from their experiences and keep moving forward.

20

Chapter 20: Social Entrepreneurship

Social entrepreneurship was a key focus for Saintly Startups. Musa and his team believed that businesses could be powerful agents of social change, addressing pressing issues and creating positive impact. They encouraged young entrepreneurs to develop ventures that prioritized social and environmental goals alongside financial success.

One notable story was that of Ibrahim, a social entrepreneur who started a recycling initiative in his community. Ibrahim's venture, EcoCycle, not only addressed the problem of waste management but also provided job opportunities for marginalized individuals. His efforts significantly improved the cleanliness and sustainability of the community.

Ibrahim's story highlighted the potential of social entrepreneurship to drive meaningful change. It demonstrated that businesses could be a force for good, solving societal challenges and contributing to the well-being of communities. The Saintly Startups movement championed social entrepreneurship, inspiring young entrepreneurs to make a difference.

21

Chapter 21: Building Strong Partnerships

Partnerships played a crucial role in the success of Saintly Startups. Musa and his team understood that collaboration and synergy were essential for achieving greater impact. They encouraged young entrepreneurs to build strong partnerships with other businesses, organizations, and stakeholders.

One memorable story was that of Bilal, an entrepreneur who partnered with a local nonprofit to provide vocational training for youth. Through this partnership, Bilal's tech startup, Innovate, offered coding and digital skills workshops to young people, empowering them with valuable skills for the future.

Bilal's story demonstrated the power of partnerships in amplifying impact. It showcased how businesses and organizations could work together to create meaningful change and achieve shared goals. The Saintly Startups movement fostered a culture of collaboration, promoting the idea that together, they could accomplish more.

22

Chapter 22: The Role of Faith-Based Networks

Faith-based networks provided a strong support system for the Saintly Startups movement. Musa and his team leveraged these networks to connect with like-minded individuals, share resources, and gain valuable insights. These networks became a source of inspiration and guidance for young entrepreneurs.

One inspiring story was that of Fatima, an entrepreneur who relied on her faith community for support and mentorship. Through her network, Fatima gained access to valuable resources and opportunities that helped her grow her sustainable fashion brand. Her faith-based network provided a sense of belonging and encouragement throughout her journey.

Fatima's story highlighted the importance of faith-based networks in entrepreneurship. It demonstrated that these networks could offer invaluable support, fostering a sense of community and shared purpose. The Saintly Startups movement leveraged faith-based networks to strengthen their initiatives and create a supportive ecosystem.

23

Chapter 23: Ethical Marketing Practices

Ethical marketing practices were a key principle for Saintly Startups. Musa and his team believed that honesty and transparency were essential in building trust with customers. They encouraged young entrepreneurs to adopt ethical marketing strategies that aligned with their values.

One notable story was that of Sarah, a young marketer who developed a campaign for a local organic food startup. Sarah's approach focused on educating consumers about the benefits of organic farming and the importance of supporting local farmers. Her honest and transparent campaign resonated with customers, building a loyal and engaged community.

Sarah's story showcased the impact of ethical marketing practices. It demonstrated that by prioritizing honesty and transparency, businesses could build strong relationships with their customers and create lasting value. The Saintly Startups movement championed ethical marketing, promoting integrity and trust in all business interactions.

24

Chapter 24: Measuring Impact

Measuring impact was an essential aspect of the Saintly Startups movement. Musa and his team believed that it was important to track the social and environmental impact of their ventures, ensuring that they were making a positive difference. They developed tools and frameworks to measure and report on their impact.

One inspiring story was that of Ahmed, an entrepreneur who started a clean energy initiative. Ahmed's venture, Solar Solutions, provided affordable solar energy to rural communities. By measuring the impact of his initiative, Ahmed was able to demonstrate the significant reduction in carbon emissions and the improvement in the quality of life for the community.

Ahmed's story highlighted the importance of measuring impact in entrepreneurship. It demonstrated that by tracking and reporting on their progress, businesses could showcase their contributions and inspire others to follow suit. The Saintly Startups movement prioritized impact measurement, ensuring that their efforts were both effective and meaningful.

25

Chapter 25: The Future of Saintly Startups

As the Saintly Startups movement continued to grow, Musa and his team looked towards the future with optimism and determination. They envisioned a world where ethical entrepreneurship was the norm, where businesses prioritized integrity, innovation, and social responsibility. They continued to inspire and support young entrepreneurs, ensuring that the legacy of Saintly Startups would endure for generations to come.

One final story was that of Musa himself, reflecting on his journey and the impact of the movement he had started. As he looked back on the countless lives that had been touched and the positive change that had been created, Musa felt a deep sense of fulfillment and purpose. He knew that the Saintly Startups movement was not just a fleeting trend but a lasting force for good.

Musa's story was a testament to the power of vision, faith, and perseverance. It demonstrated that with the right values and a commitment to making a difference, entrepreneurs could create businesses that were both successful and meaningful. The future of Saintly Startups was bright, and its impact would continue to ripple across communities, inspiring a new generation of ethical entrepreneurs.

Book Description: Saintly Startups: Encouraging Faith, Ethics, and Innovation in Young Minds

In the vibrant town of Suleja, a unique entrepreneurial movement is taking root—one that harmonizes faith, ethics, and innovation. "Saintly Startups" weaves an inspiring narrative of young minds driven by a divine calling to create businesses that prioritize integrity and social responsibility over sheer profit.

Through the eyes of visionary leader Musa, this book captures the essence of ethical entrepreneurship. From the creation of an "Ethical Entrepreneur's Handbook" to the fusion of faith and cutting-edge innovation, each chapter is brimming with real-life stories of resilience, empathy, and community-driven change. Follow the journeys of characters like Mariam, who designs eco-friendly packaging, and Ibrahim, who pioneers faith-driven financial models, as they navigate the challenges and triumphs of building sustainable and impactful ventures.

"Saintly Startups" not only celebrates the successes of these young entrepreneurs but also delves into the importance of mentorship, education, and embracing diversity. It emphasizes the role of faith as a guiding light in business decisions and showcases the transformative power of social entrepreneurship.

With compelling anecdotes and practical wisdom, this book is a testament to the belief that true success lies in making a positive difference in the world. "Saintly Startups" is a beacon of hope for aspiring entrepreneurs, illustrating that with faith, ethics, and innovation, the journey to meaningful and lasting impact is not only possible but deeply fulfilling.

Embark on this inspiring journey and discover how the next generation of entrepreneurs is creating a brighter, more ethical future for us all.